In case

As a reward: $